ANDET
LADUGÅRDSVIKEN
DJURGÅRDEN
Lustholmen
Notholmen
Blekholmen
SALTSJÖN

FACTS CHECKED BY THE VASA MUSEUM IN STOCKHOLM

MIX
Paper from responsible sources
FSC® C015559

Rabén & Sjögren
Box 2052, SE-103 12 Stockholm
rabensjogren.se

Translation Lars Norén
First edition. Fifth printing
Printed in Poland 2014
ISBN 978-91-29-65905-4

Rabén & Sjögren is part of
Norstedts Publishing Group

Björn Bergenholtz

The Vasa Piglet

Translated by Lars Norén

PIGLET LINDBOM'S ADVENTURES
ON BOARD THE ROYAL WARSHIP VASA

rabén&sjögren

THE YEAR
1628
IN THE KINGDOM OF SWEDEN´S CAPITAL
STOCKHOLM

Once upon a time there was a king. Like a lot of kings at this time he occasionally went to war. And now this particular king was fighting a war against his rebellious cousin Sigismund, king of Poland. For this war the Swedish king had had a new ship built. The Vasa was bigger and shapelier, and had more guns than other warships.

At this time there was also a piglet. And this particular piglet was called Lindbom. Piglet Lindbom and his family lived on a farm, in Ladugårdslandet, a mile or two from the Royal Palace. If he tried, Piglet Lindbom could make out the palace's towers and golden spires, in the distance. But little pigs don't enjoy gold and kings that much. Mud puddles, now that's fun!

The sun was out and the mud puddle was nice and warm. None of the pigs gave a second thought to the stranger who was leaning on the fence. He looked rather grim, this man, and he was talking to Pig Farmer John, who owned the farm. Piglet Lindbom wasn't really listening, not until the stranger pointed at him.

"I'll have that one. The one with the droopy ear. Not too fat, not too lean."

"It's a nice little pig," said Farmer John. "The price is three Daler."

"Exorbitant!" the man snarled. "I'll give you two."

And that's how Piglet Lindbom suddenly got a new master, and would now end up somewhere else.

With a rope around Piglet Lindbom's neck, the grim-looking man set off at a brisk pace towards town. Maybe not that brisk, come to think of it, as Piglet Lindbom was pulling the other way. Still, there's can do to stop a fully grown man.

They walked along Katthavet, passed the King's Garden and reached the city gates, on the islets north of the Palace.

"Delivery to His Majesty's Ship!" called the grim man to the guards. They were let into the city of Stockholm. The town was chock-a-block. People milling around everywhere. And the narrow alleys carried wafts of rubbish, beer and chamber-pots.

Moored below the King's Palace was an enormous ship. "Behold the Vasa!" exclaimed the grim man. "Have you ever seen a more magnificent ship?"

Piglet Lindbom looked at the ship and turned up his snout. "Guns and gargoyles. I'm no sailor, I'm a pig. Why should I go on that ship?!" thought Piglet Lindbom.

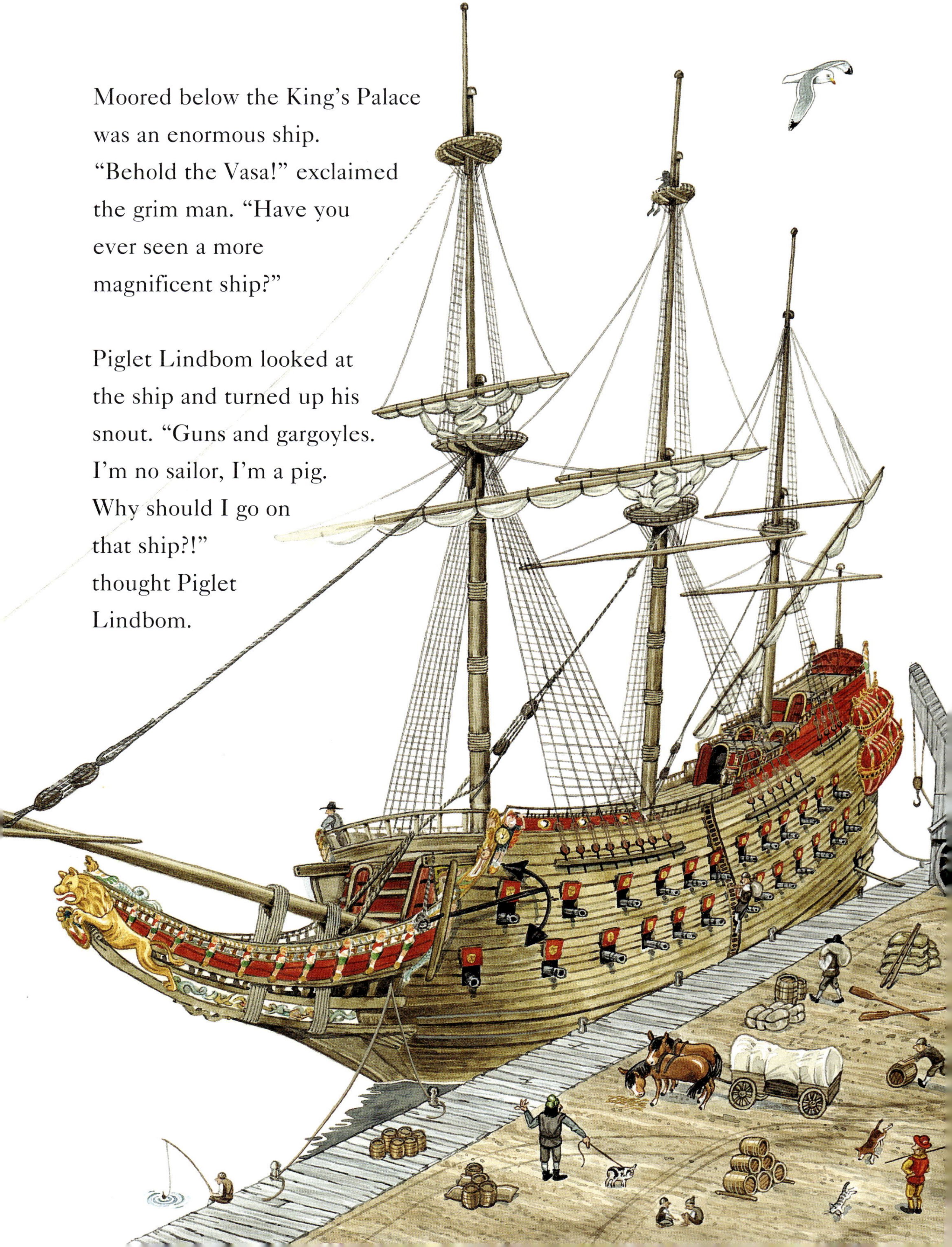

The man grabbed the little pig and hurled him through a hatch in the side of the ship. Piglet Lindbom landed with a thud on the floor. He blinked and tried to get used to the dingy light. The grim man climbed through the hatch and dragged Piglet Lindbom down into the ship. It was cold and dark. Like a cave. And there was a smell of sea water.

Waiting by a huge cauldron were two men. One of them sucking a small pipe, and the other sharpening a knife.

"Cook, I've brought you the vice-admiral's piglet."

Confused, Lindbom looked at the two men by the cauldron. The man with the pipe slowly blew a ring of smoke. The cook stopped sharpening his knife and began to scratch his nose.

"With a bit of sage you'll make quite a cutlet," he said grinning.

"They're going to have me for their dinner!" Lindbom thought.

"An ice-amdiral is going to eat me!"

As fast as his little piggy-trotters would carry him, Piglet Lindbom fled further into the dark ship. Echoing from the galley, he could hear the men's hearty laughter.

Lindbom hid right at the back of the ship, among cannonballs and beer barrels. He felt terribly small and terribly lonely.

Then, in the darkest corner, there was a glimmer of something. Piglet Lindbom looked again. Yes, there was something. Something blinking! Eyes! Someone was staring at him.
"What's the matter with you?" said a voice, suddenly.

“What are you sitting here for, sourpuss?”
Out of the darkness a nosy-looking
rat came towards him.
“I’m not a puss. I’m a pig,”
Lindbom said. “An ice-amdiral
wants to eat me. I have to escape, but
I don’t know how to.”

“Nothing to it,” said the rat, polishing her whiskers.
“You just creep up on deck, drop into the drink and
swim ashore. Easy as pie.”

With a swift movement the rat was gone, leaving the little pig on his own. "Easy as pie," Lindbom thought. "Maybe if you're a rat, but piglets aren't very good swimmers." Piglet Lindbom went over to the ladder. Pigs aren't very good climbers, either, but there was no other way out. On wobbly legs he made his way up to the gun deck.

On gun deck there were rows and rows of guns. Huddled between them were small groups of sailors. They looked anxious and were whispering. Rumour had it that in a dream the king had seen the Vasa sink. Someone made a slurping noise and one of the men coughed, with wheezing lungs. No one noticed the little pig silently slipping past.

Out on deck there was a slight breeze and the sun was slowly setting. A little further along, a man was waiting for a catch. A fat cat next to him was waiting for the same thing.

The cat caught sight of Piglet Lindbom.
"Ship ahoy! What have I spotted? A land-lubber," the ship's cat said with a snigger.
"I'm not a lubber. I'm a pig," Lindbom said.
"As you like," said the cat. But listen, that old geezer won't be catching any fish. Are you hungry?"
Piglet Lindbom nodded.
"Come on, I know where there's food," the cat said and was off.
Lindbom followed suit.

They crept into the captain's cabin. A few noble-looking men were gathered round a table. A bit of sausage and a blob or two of pickled cabbage lay on the floor. The men's table manners weren't so noble.

"But what's a pig doing on board?" the cat whispered, her mouth full of sausage.

"An ice-amdiral is going to have me for his dinner," Piglet Lindbom answered in a sad whisper.

"Oh, I see!" said the cat. "It's him, there."

The cat pointed at a pair of thin legs sticking out under the table. Lindbom turned white with fear. Then he got angry. And bit one of the thin legs – hard! The vice-admiral screamed, the table crashed to the floor, and Lindbom was flung out on deck, like a shot.

Now Lindbom was in a pickle. Where should he hide? Up the mast! And forgetting that pigs can't climb rigs, Piglet Lindbom made his way up the mast.

Out of breath and with trembling legs, Piglet Lindbom hid way up in the main mast. Below, the city lay dark and still. Here and there a glimmering lantern shone, and the rattling of the city guards' swords filtered through the alleys.

The moon lit up a clear sky and way up above there was a shooting star. Farmer John used to say you could make a wish when you saw a shooting star.

Piglet Lindbom closed his eyes and wished that, some way, he could leave the ship. Only now he was too tired to think about it. Lindbom yawned, curled up and fell asleep. Safe, for the moment – way, way up above deck.

Then came morning. It was Sunday 10th August, the day when dreams come true, according to popular belief. Piglet Lindbom woke up and squinted at the sun, which was already high in the sky. It was a glorious morning. Providing you´re not going to be eaten up, of course.

Down on deck there were loads of people. They looked like ants. The vice-admiral looked like a particularly colourful ant. With a bandage round one leg.

Everywhere were sailors preparing to set sail. And nowhere an escape route for Piglet Lindbom.

There was a tear in the corner of the piglet's eye.
"What kind of a crybaby are you?" a voice suddenly said. It was a seagull.
"I'm not a baby," Lindbom sniffled. "I'm a pig. And I don't know how to get out of here."
"Well, I never ...," laughed the gull. "Copy me. Fly!" The seagull winged round and vanished across the water.
Piglet Lindbom sighed and thought: "Seagulls don't know much about pigs."

From the ship below loud voices were calling. It was time to cast off.

As the wind blew the wrong way the men – heaving and puffing – had to pull the gigantic ship a bit along the way. But soon the master could order the sails to be set. The sailors entered the rig. Soon some of them reached Piglet Lindbom, who tried to make himself look as small as possible.

There was a creaking and a squeaking of rigging and ropes. When the sails filled, the mast gave a jerk. Piglet Lindbom lost his grip. And fell!

He managed to grab hold of a rope, spun round, bounced against the rigging and kept falling through the air.

At the last moment he got a grip on one of the guns. With a dizzy head he climbed up on the barrel. Above him, the sails curved lightly in the wind.

And then the ship started moving. The Vasa was under sail! In a slow and dignified fashion she began floating out to sea. Along the shores thousands of Stockholmers were gathered. They were shouting and cheering.

The ship responded by firing four crashingly loud salvos. “A crash and a bang,” muttered Piglet Lindbom and covered his ears. The people on land were exultant and waved even more. Lindbom didn’t bother to return the waving. He was fed up with this stupid boat.

After only a few hundred metres a gust of wind made the ship keel over. Piglet Lindbom nearly slid off the gun barrel, but the ship righted itself. Suddenly, it was absolutely quiet on board. Only the creaking of the masts could be heard. Then there was another gust of wind, a little stronger than before. The Vasa keeled over alarmingly.

The people on deck fell over. And the sailors up in the rig held on for dear life. The captain shouted: "Cast off all topsail sheets!"

But it was too late. Water gushed in through the open gun ports. The Vasa started sinking. Lindbom looked around for something to keep him afloat. The men up in the masts let go and threw themselves into the air. Shouts and prayers and men cursing and calling for help could be heard from the ship. Along the shores the many thousand Stockholmers had gone quiet. They were horrified to see the great ship sinking.

The King's ship had sunk to the bottom of the sea. Luckily it wasn't very deep and two of the masts stuck up above water. Many of the crew clung to them. Boats from every direction hurried to lend a helping hand to those who had ended up in the water.

Piglet Lindbom climbed up on the mizzenmast. It had broken off when the ship went down and now it was bobbing up and down in the water.

Thus, perched on the mast, Piglet Lindbom was gently floating away in the evening sun. Safe and happy. He would never be anyone's dinner. Never ever.

THE END

This is where Pig Lindbom lived.
Royal Dramatic Theatre
NORRMALM
Sergels torg
King's Garden
Nybroviken
Royal Palace
The Vasa is pulled along using manpower.
Town Hall
RIDDARHOLMEN
OLD TOWN
Riddarfjärden
Sails are set.
Katarinahissen
SÖDERMALM

STOCKHOLM